American Girl®

ULTIMATE STICKER COLLECTION

Dress up

How to use this book

Read the captions, then find the sticker that best fits the space.
(Hint: check the bold sticker labels for clues!)

There are lots of fantastic extra stickers for creating
your own scenes throughout the book.

DK | Penguin Random House

Written and edited by Lisa Stock
Designed by David McDonald

This American Edition, 2023
First American Edition, 2017
Published in the United States by DK Publishing
1745 Broadway, 20th Floor, New York, NY 10019

Page design copyright © 2023 Dorling Kindersley Limited
DK, a Division of Penguin Random House LLC
23 24 25 26 10 9 8 7 6 5 4 3 2 1
001–333948–05/2023

A catalog record for this book is available from
the Library of Congress.

ISBN: 978-0-7440-7377-5

DK books are available at special discounts when
purchased in bulk for sales promotions, premiums,
fund-raising, or educational use. For details, contact:
DK Publishing Special Markets,
1745 Broadway, 20th Floor, New York, NY 10019
SpecialSales@dk.com

Printed and bound in China

www.americangirl.com

For the curious

www.dk.com

FSC
MIX
Paper | Supporting
responsible forestry
FSC™ C018179

This book was made with Forest
Stewardship Council™ certified
paper—one small step in DK's
commitment to a sustainable future.
For more information go to
www.dk.com/our-green-pledge

T0286252

Standout style

Each American Girl® character has her own individual look. The one thing they all have in common is that they all look super stylish!

Groovy vest

Bell-bottom jeans

1974

Flower power
Julie's style is far out! She loves bright colors, flower patterns, and cool braids in her hair.

Platform sandals

≈ 1764 ≈

Little details
Kaya's dress has lots of pretty fringing, beads, and a tie belt. Her moccasins keep her feet warm and dry.

Hair ties

Cloche hat

Fringed dress

≈ 1934 ≈

Dress to impress
Kit's ready for a day out in her charming floral dress. Her matching bracelet, hat, and purse finish the look.

Flowery dress

Red strappy shoes

3

All dressed up

The girls love special occasions. Whether it's a prom, a performance, or a trip to church, they can't wait to put on their best outfits.

Pink bow barrette

Lace gloves

~1954~
Prom parade
Maryellen feels so grown up when she tries on her sister's pink prom dress. She hopes it will help her stand out from the crowd.

Embroidered tulle skirt

White patent shoes

~ 1964 ~

Sunday best

Melody is ready to sing her heart out in the choir on Easter Sunday. Her bright-green daisy-covered dress is perfect for spring!

Orchid hair clip

Pleated skirt

Patterned knee socks

~ 1941 ~

Traditional dress

Nanea wears a special holoku dress with a long train when she performs a dance for the United States Armed Forces.

Lei made from maile leaves

5

Favorite things

Stretchy workout gear, patriotic camp clothes, or a home game uniform—each of the girls has a special outfit for her favorite hobby.

Sweatband

Cropped sweatshirt

Printed leotard

Knit leg warmers

1986

Work it out!

When Courtney wants to work out with her mom she wears this cool aerobics outfit and plays a video on the TV.

Baseball cap

1944

Happy camper

Molly loves her summers at Camp Gowonagin. Every morning the campers wear their uniforms to the flag-raising ceremony.

Team logo

Pleated shorts

Sports shorts

Navy saddle shoes

1974

Ball time

Julie's favorite sport is basketball. When her team, the Jaguars, plays on its home court her teammates wear this uniform.

Lace-up shoes

Winter warmers

In the wintertime, the girls put on their warmest clothes and wrap up against the cold. Out in the snow, they look snug and stylish!

1864

Winter wear
Addy's winter coat has a cute plaid trim. Her coat, hat, and boots keep her warm on the chilly walk to church.

Derby hat

Thick green coat

Practical winter shoes

Purple hat

1914

Fancy coat
Keeping warm in the New York winters is easy for Rebecca, with her purple and white winter coat and matching hat.

Faux-fur trim

Velveteen swing coat

White shoes

Woolen snow pants

1954

Sledding
Maryellen's hat, plaid jacket, and waterproof boots keep her warm and cozy when she goes sledding for the very first time!

Rain boots

Schooltime

The girls always make sure they look neat and tidy in the classroom. Knee-length skirts, bright colors, and shiny shoes are pretty and practical.

Red satin bow

Short-sleeved cardigan

⚬1954⚬

Class style
Maryellen picks this outfit to start the new school year in. The Peter Pan collar and bow-print dress make it extra special.

Bow-print dress

Polka-dot ribbon bows

1964

School days
Melody wears a jumper and striped shirt to school. Every Monday, she and her friend Sharon wear matching-colored hair ribbons.

1944

Perfect in plaid
Molly loves everything about third grade! On school days she wears a white blouse and a plaid jumper with a pleated skirt.

Red silky hairbows

Green hair ribbon

Plaid jumper

Sleeveless jumper

White ankle socks

Red tights

11

Sweet dreams

When the sun sets it's time for the girls to get ready for bed. In their favorite pajamas, they are sure to have a good night's sleep.

Satin bow

City sleep
Rebecca finds this nightgown perfect for a cool night in her New York City apartment.

1914

Nightgown

Fluffy slippers

Silk head wrap

1941

Perfect pajamas
Claudie wears yellow pajamas decorated with purple flowers. The soft cotton keeps her comfy while she sleeps.

Floral-print PJs

Dog and balloon print

1954

Puppy PJs
Maryellen has a nightly reminder of her adorable dachshund, Scooter, with this dog-patterned bedtime-wear.

Bunny slippers

Moccasin slippers

Furry friends

Pets come in different shapes and sizes, and all of them can be a BFF! Loyal and loving, these animals would do anything for their owners.

⊰ 1922 ⊱
Dizzy Dot
Claudie and her brother love to play with this mixed-breed pup. She belongs to the boardinghouse manager, Miss Amelia.

Pink bow

Long fur

Saddle pad

~1764~

Steps High
Kaya's beloved horse has a saddle with colorful side panels and a fringed blanket that sits underneath.

Scruffy gray fur

Fringed blanket

Blue ribbon

~1941~

Mele
Nanea's dog, Mele, has scruffy gray fur and wears a blue collar that makes her instantly recognizable.

In the spotlight

For creative girls, there's nothing better than a fun-filled day of music and dancing! They choose outfits that will help them shine.

Flower lei

Feathered ʻuliʻuli rattle

Hula

Nanea has been taking hula classes since she was little. She loves wearing clothes that honor the beautiful traditions of Hawaii.

Ti-leaf skirt

Doo-wop
Melody dreams of singing backup for her brother. Her pink sequinned dress and elegant silky gloves make her feel like a star.

Satin headband

White capelet

Fringed skirt

Pink slip-on shoes

Jazz style
Claudie gets to wear this fabulous flapper-style outfit when she takes tap classes with her best friend, Nina.

Black ruffles

Silver tap shoes

17

Use your extra stickers to fill the scene with your favorite dolls!

18

19

Starry night

When it starts to get dark, that's the cue to put on some soft and cozy PJs, make some warm cocoa, and get ready for some snuggling up!

Corinne

Corinne keeps the mountains close to her even while she's indoors with her powder blue printed PJs.

Hooded sweatshirt

Fleece shorts

Knit slipper socks

Travel in style

Jetting off around the world can lead to so many adventures ... and having the perfect outfit to wear for the trip can make it even better!

Straw hat

Colorful swimsuit

Woven beach bag

Draped sarong

Pink sandals

Beach day

Heading to the beach on a hot day calls for a swimsuit and cute sarong cover-up. Don't forget to pack a sun hat!

Pink beret

Off to Paris
Outfits can be inspired by glamorous locations! This Eiffel Tower-print blouse is the perfect reminder of beautiful Paris.

Pilot's hat

Bouclé skirt

Sparkly pink hearts

Navy suit

Up and away
An airline captain's uniform lets passengers know who's in charge of the plane. This dark-navy suit is brightened up by a pink neck scarf.

23

Sports day

For sporty girls who love to be on a basketball court, a soccer pitch, or performing somersaults, stylish sportswear is a must!

Red-and-white hairband

Red-and-white pom-poms

Cheer jersey

Ra-ra ready
This bright cheerleading uniform and pom-poms are just the thing to bring team spirit to any big game.

White sneakers

Perfect routine
Who wouldn't flip for this plum gymnastics leotard? Covered with silver swirls, it's eye-catching as well as comfy.

Elastic headband

Soccer jersey

Long-sleeved leotard

Satin slippers

Soccer shorts

Go for goal
A team soccer jersey, shorts, and knee socks are perfect for soccer practice or for game days.

Ball

Sleepover fun

What could be more fun than a sleepover with best friends? Games, giggles, and a pajama fashion show will make for a night to remember!

Tie-dyed jumpsuit

Pink furry slippers

Fluffy pillow

Bright-pink jogger pants

Multicolored pom-poms

Birthday party

The birthday girl is always the center of attention at her own party! A sash and party hat make it clear to everyone whose big day it is!

Gift-shaped party hat

Balloon

Rainbow layered cake

Sparkly party dress

Cupcake

Birthday cake cart

Lace-up sneakers

Perfect pets

While some animal playmates keep busy playing with yarn or chewing toys, others have important jobs to do to help those around them!

Sturdy handle

Service dog

This pup loves to lend a helping paw. His bright-orange service-dog vest makes his special job clear to everyone.

Shiny medal

Multicolored fur

Pastel kitty
Purrply Pink Kitty has a personality that's as sweet as she looks! She loves playing with her ball of soft blue yarn.

Yarn toy

Golden-brown fur

Daffodil Doodle
With his adorable curly golden-brown fur and brown eyes, how can anyone resist playing with Daffodil?

Barbell toy

Spa day

Ready for some me-time? A little rest and relaxation can be just the tonic. Grab a robe or some yoga gear, breathe deeply, and stretch!

Pink headband

AMERICAN GIRL
HOTEL & SPA

Yoga mat

Deep breaths

This cute and calm yoga outfit can help anyone feel centered. It's super fashionable, too!

Tank top and cardigan

Animal-print leggings

Zen zone
Comfy leggings and a tank top blooming with a pink lotus flower bring a very peaceful vibe to this look.

Cloth headband

Green tank top

Pink-trimmed robe

Lotus-print leggings

Gold strappy sandals

Pamper day
It's time to kick back and relax in a simple soft robe and sliders. Perfect for a day of pampering!

Slide-on sandals

31

Use your extra stickers to fill the scene with your favorite dolls!

32

Groovy vest

Bell-bottom jeans

Platform sandals

Hair ties

Cloche hat

Flowery dress

Fringed dress

Red strappy shoes

Patterned knee socks

Lei made from maile leaves

Pleated skirt

Orchid hair clip

Lace gloves

White patent shoes

Embroidered tulle skirt

Pink bow barrette

Stickers for pages 6–7

Sweatband

Team logo

Cropped sweatshirt

Printed leotard

Sports shorts

Knit leg warmers

Lace-up shoes

Navy saddle shoes

Baseball cap

Pleated shorts

White shoes

Purple hat

Faux-fur trim

Derby hat

Velveteen swing coat

Woolen snow pants

Rain boots

Thick green coat

Practical winter shoes

Short-sleeved cardigan

Sleeveless jumper

Bow-print dress

Red silky hairbows

Polka-dot ribbon bows

Red satin bow

Red tights

Green hair ribbon

White ankle socks

Plaid jumper

Nightgown

Bunny slippers

Floral-print PJs

Satin bow

Fluffy slippers

Silk head wrap

Moccasin slippers

Dog and balloon print

Blue ribbon

Saddle pad

Pink bow

Long fur

Scruffy gray fur

Feathered
'uli'uli rattle

Ti-leaf
skirt

Fringed skirt

Satin
headband

White
capelet

Pink
slip-on
shoes

Silver tap shoes

Black ruffles

Flower lei

Fleece shorts

Hooded sweatshirt

Snowflake design

Button-down top

Knit slipper socks

Wide leg PJ pants

PJ pants drawstring

Multicolored fuzzy slippers

Blue PJ T-shirt

Sparkly pink hearts

Bouclé skirt

Pilot's hat

Woven beach bag

Pink beret

Navy suit

Draped sarong

Straw hat

Pink sandals

Colorful swimsuit

Stickers for pages 24–25

Satin slippers

Red-and-white hairband

White sneakers

Long-sleeved leotard

Cheer jersey

Red-and-white pom-poms

Ball

Soccer jersey

Soccer shorts

©/™ 2023 American Girl

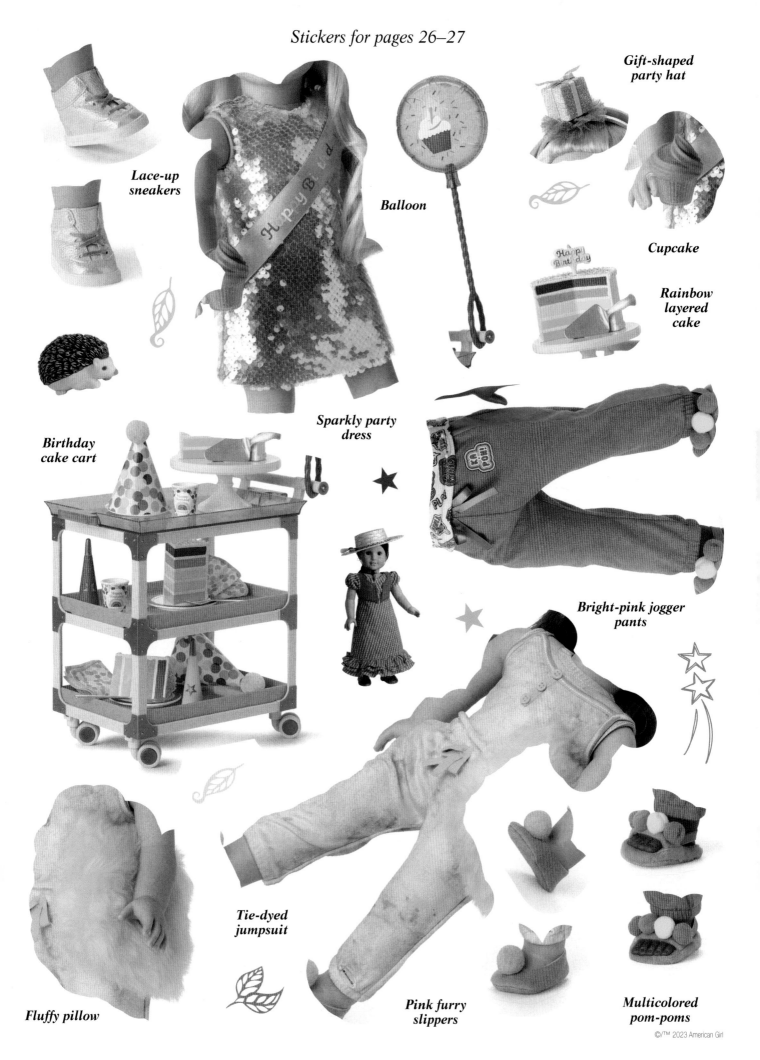

Stickers for pages 26–27

Lace-up
sneakers

Balloon

Gift-shaped
party hat

Cupcake

Rainbow
layered
cake

Sparkly party
dress

Birthday
cake cart

Bright-pink jogger
pants

Tie-dyed
jumpsuit

Fluffy pillow

Pink furry
slippers

Multicolored
pom-poms

©/™ 2023 American Girl

Stickers for pages 28–29

Yarn toy

Shiny medal

Barbell toy

Sturdy handle

Multicolored fur

Stickers for pages 30–31

Pink headband

Gold strappy sandals

Green tank top

Yoga mat

Cloth headband

Tank top and cardigan

Lotus-print leggings

Pink-trimmed robe

Animal-print leggings

Slide-on sandals

©/™ 2023 American Girl

Extra stickers

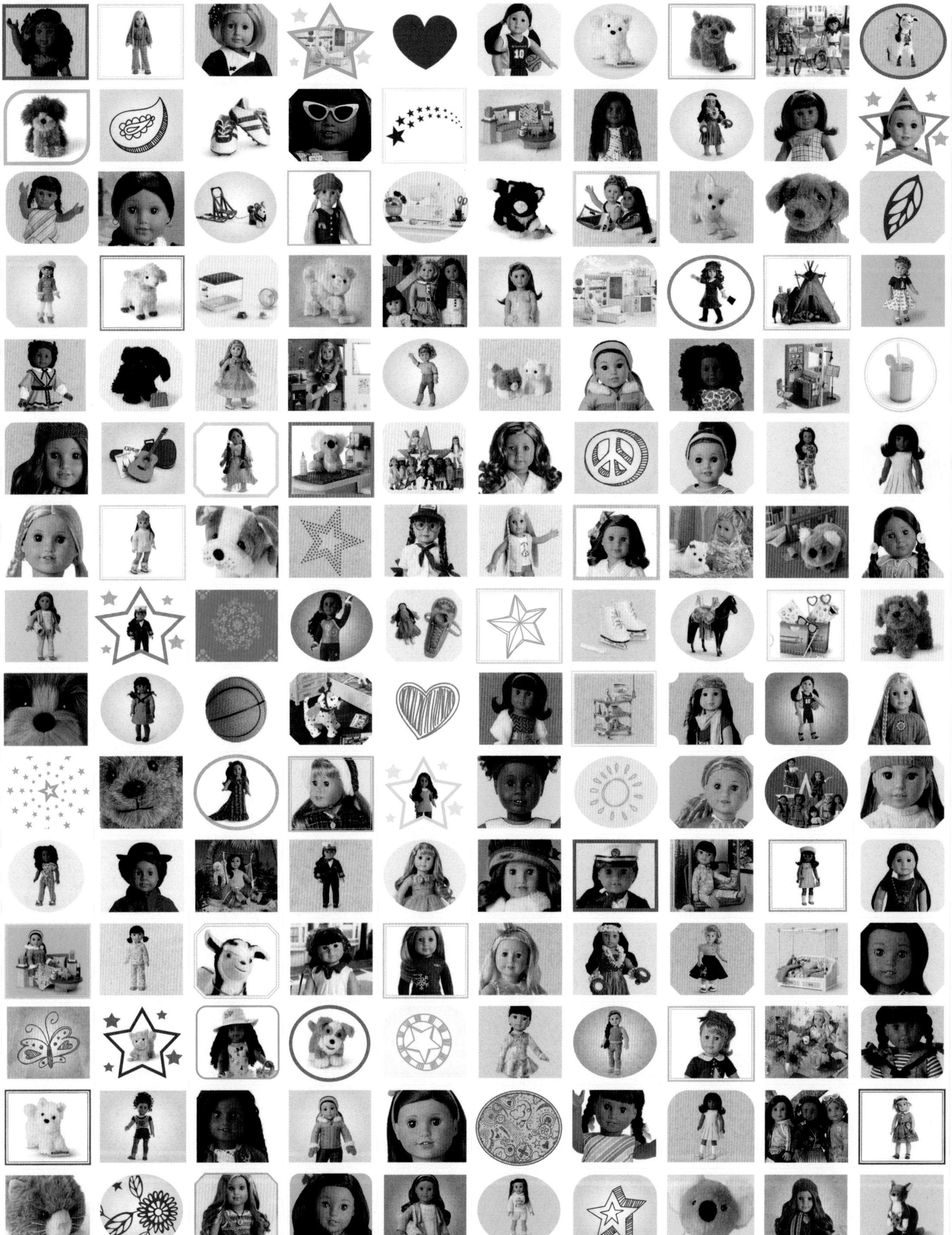

Extra stickers

Extra stickers

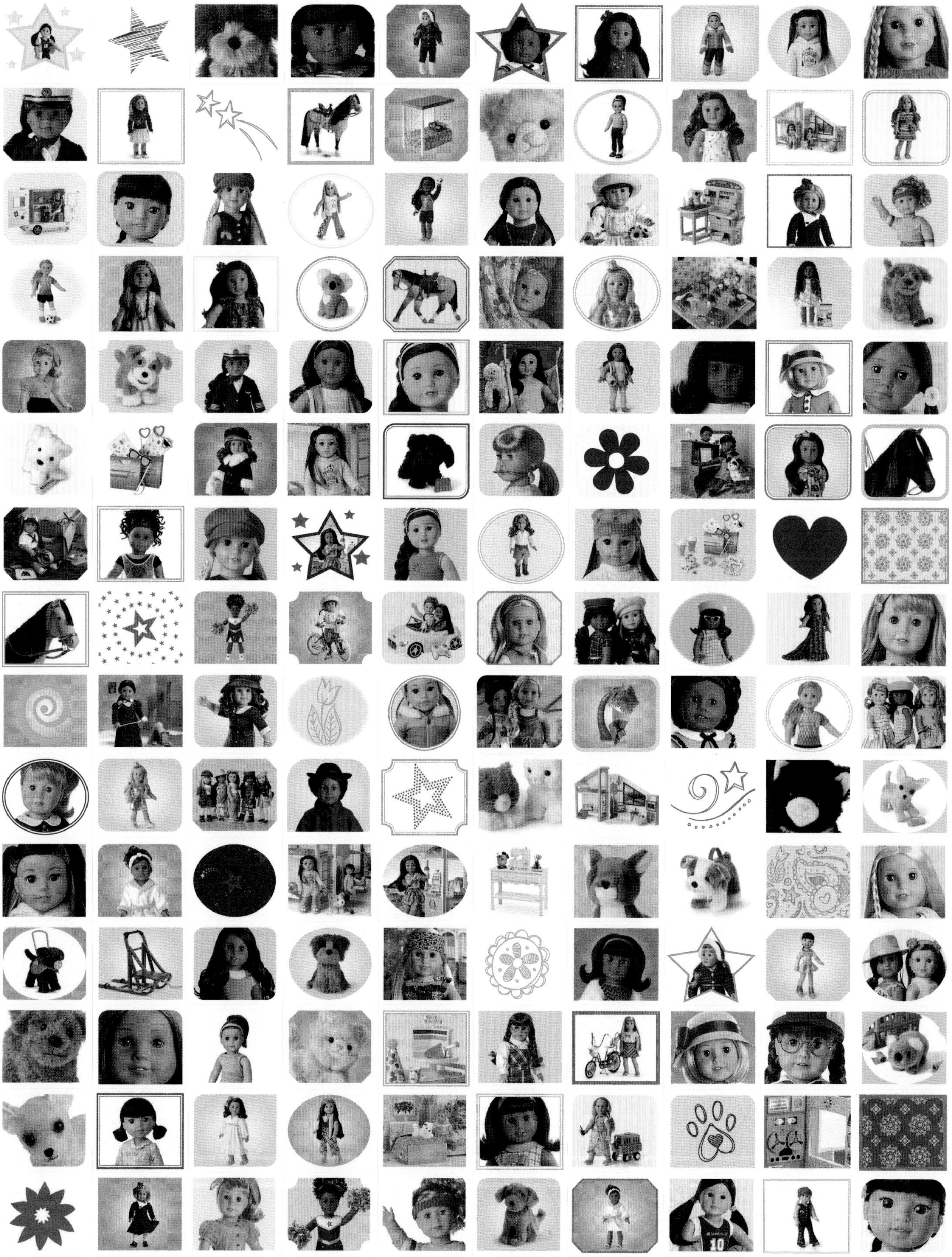

Extra stickers

Extra stickers

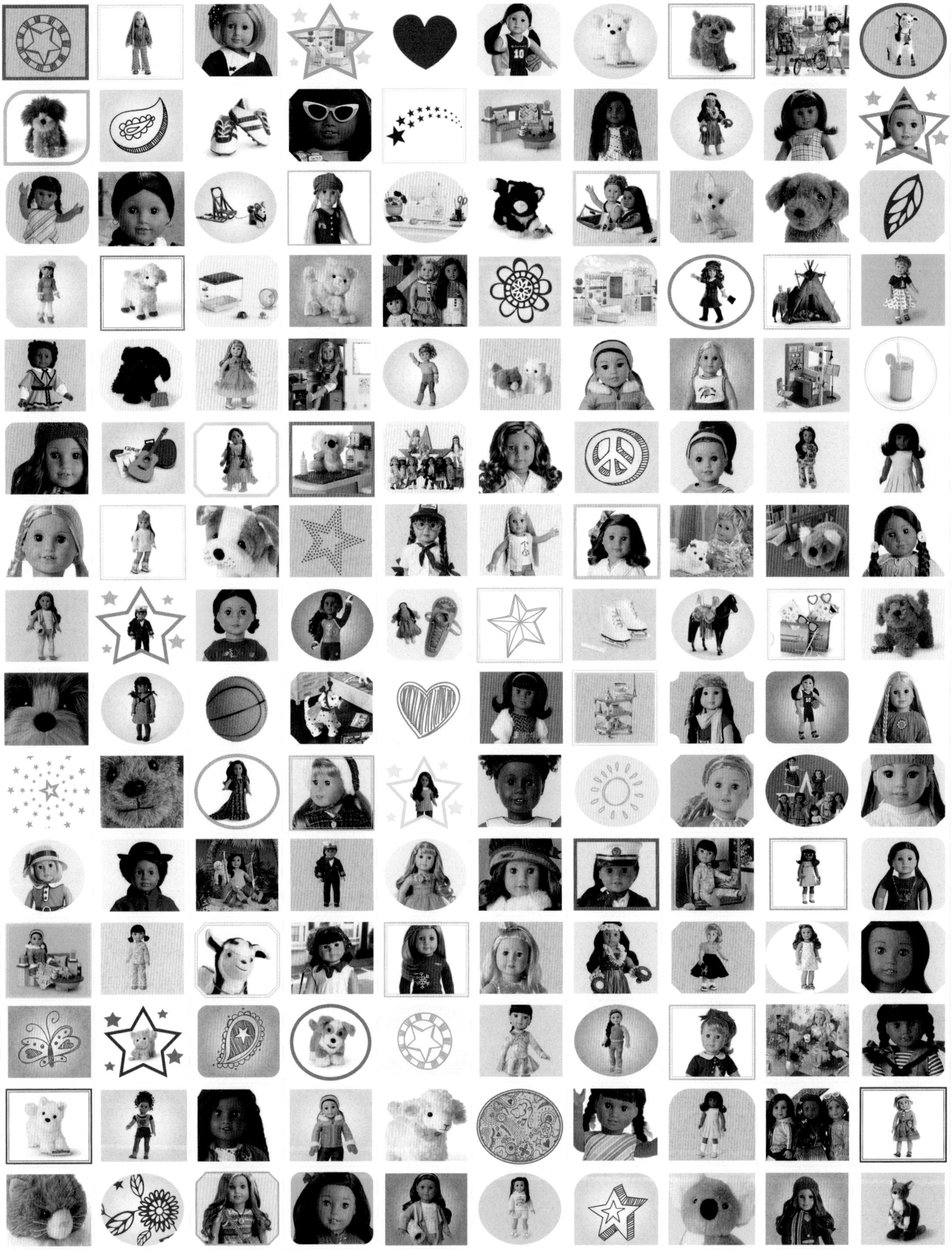

Extra stickers

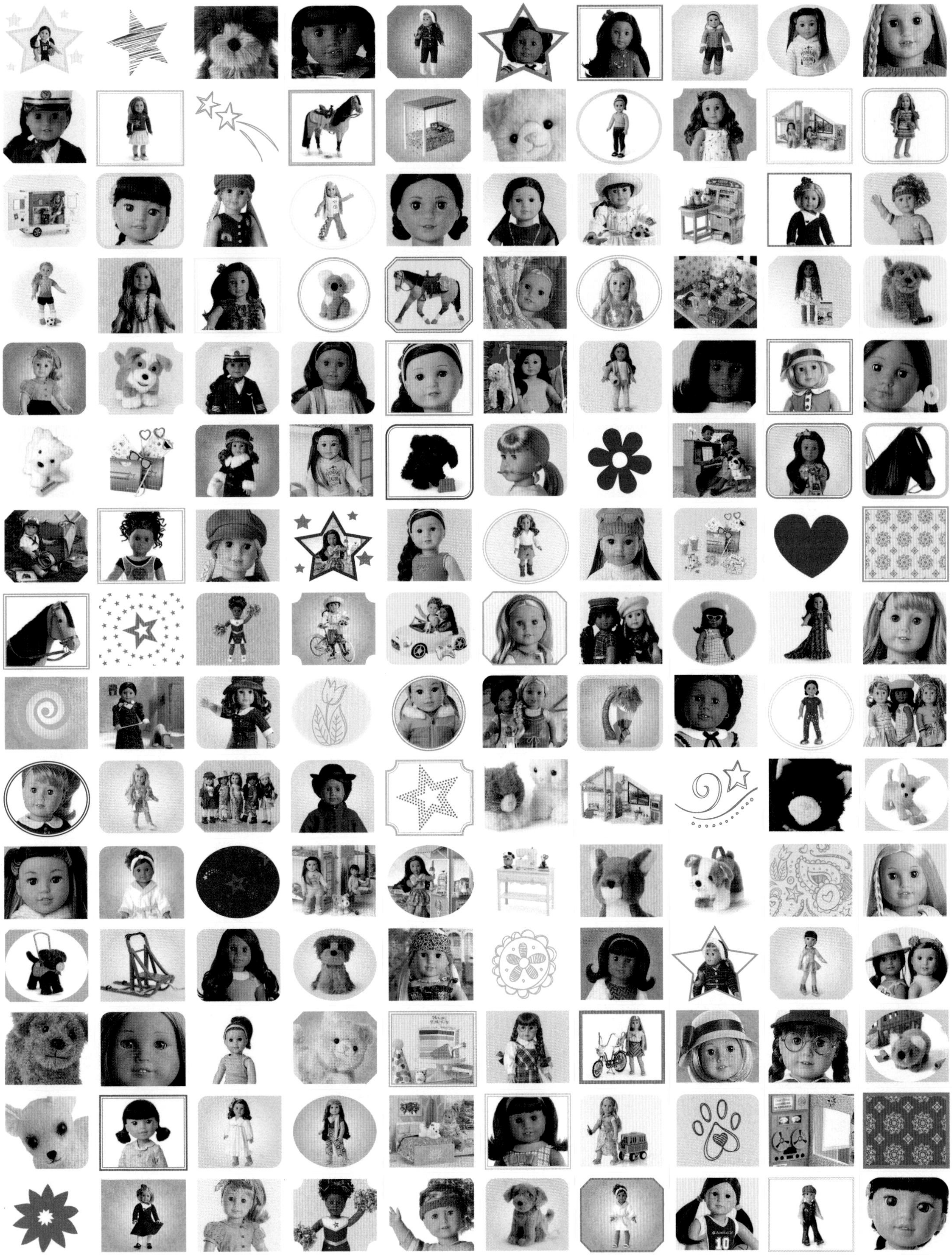